Working Together Against
DRINKING
AND DRIVING

Many teens are becoming actively involved in the fight against drinking and driving.

❖ THE LIBRARY OF SOCIAL ACTIVISM ❖

Working Together Against

DRINKING AND DRIVING

Janet Grosshandler-Smith

THE ROSEN PUBLISHING GROUP, INC.
NEW YORK

Published in 1996 by The Rosen Publishing Group, Inc.
29 East 21st Street, New York, NY 10010

First Edition

Library of Congress Cataloging-in-Publication Data

Grosshandler, Janet.
    Working together against drinking and driving / by Janet Grosshandler-Smith
        p.   cm. — (The library of social activism)
    Includes bibliographical references and index.
    Summary: Examines the effects of drinking on driving and suggests ways you can help fight drunk driving.
        ISBN 0-8239-2259-6
        1. Drinking and traffic accidents—Juvenile literature.
    2. Traffic safety—Juvenile literature.   [1. Drinking and traffic accidents.   2. Drunk driving.   3. Traffic safety.   4. Social action.]   I. Title.   II. Series.
    HE5620.D7G763   1996
    363.12′51—dc20   96-6914
                                                                    CIP
                                                                    AC

Manufactured in the United States of America

Contents

Many teens mistakenly believe they need alcohol to have a good time.

chapter

1

THE ACCIDENT

AFTER THE CRASH, THERE WAS A STUNNED moment of silence. Then the screams could be heard from both cars involved in the head-on collision.

"Help me! Please, someone HELP ME!"

"Kim? Kim? Where's Kim?"

"Daddy! Daddy! My leg. It's bleeding."

It took four minutes for the first police car to arrive at the scene of the prom night accident. It was the longest four minutes in the lives of the people in the two battered cars.

Brian, his girlfriend Kim, and their friends, Chris and Anita, had a great time at the prom. It was the biggest night for all of them before they graduated and went their separate ways to summer jobs and college. It was also supposed to be the best. Now it had become their worst nightmare.

Brian was the only one able to get out of the car. He looked around to find Kim. But Kim had gone through the windshield. She lay face down on the smashed hood of his car, motionless, with blood all over her silver prom dress.

Anita screamed from the back seat. "I can't move! Help me! Kim! Why won't she answer me?"

The paramedics arrived and quickly began to assess the damage. Two teenagers were trapped in the car, while one lay lifeless on the hood of the car. Brian was holding a bandage to his bleeding head while he answered the police officer's questions, trying to make sense of what had happened in that split second when he lost control of his car.

Anita and Chris were in the back seat, wedged in and hurt. Kim was beyond hope. More emergency workers arrived. Fire trucks, ambulances, and more police and medical people came to help.

A man, cut and bleeding from his head, staggered from the other car. He began yelling at Brian for crashing into him and his two children. A little boy was being pulled from the station wagon. The emergency technicians started performing CPR on him.

"It's all right, Anita, we'll have you out of here soon," rescue workers repeated over and over again to the crying Anita. Machinery was brought in to cut off the roof of Brian's car. There was no other way to get Chris and Anita out. Backboards were used to lift them out.

A blanket was thrown over Kim, covering her head.

"No!" screamed Brian. Only an hour before, they had been dancing together, having the time of their *lives. He hadn't had that much to drink, had he? The bottle he had snuck into the prom was empty now, but he had just wanted a little buzz to enjoy himself more.*

The little boy was lifted from the other car into an ambulance, with rescue workers still performing CPR *on him. The anguished father held his little girl. She cried as the paramedic said soothing things to her and bandaged up her cuts.*

Another ambulance came. Anita and Chris were lifted into it.

*Brian was the least injured. He had to perform various tests for the police to determine how sober he was. He went to the hospital in the police car. There they would draw blood to find out his blood alcohol content (*BAC*). Then he would probably be charged with several crimes for drinking and driving.*

The wait for the last ambulance to take the man and his little girl to the hospital seemed to take ages. The final vehicle to arrive was the coroner's hearse. He examined Kim and pronounced her dead at the scene of the accident. The police had to find her parents and ask them to come to the morgue to identify their daughter. They had said good-bye to her only a few hours before.

The incident above was actually a mock accident. It was performed in front of the juniors and seniors of Jackson Memorial High

Mock accidents help teens understand the great personal cost of real accidents such as this one.

School a week before the Senior Prom. To show the deadly results of drinking and driving, the Jackson Township Municipal Alliance, in conjunction with Project Prom, staged this ghastly and graphic "accident." They wanted to show the students what could happen to them and their friends if they chose to drink and drive.

Volunteer students Brian, Kim, Anita, and Chris, along with a teacher and two children of other faculty members, joined with rescue workers and thirteen emergency vehicles and volunteers, to present the shocking scenes that shocked many of the students watching.

After the very realistic "accident," the stu-

dents listened to several speeches. They heard speakers from the trauma unit of a rehabilitation hospital and the mother of a Jackson Memorial High School student whose daughter had been killed by a drunk driver. A lawyer and others also spoke about what is involved in this kind of tragedy.

Kim, Anita, and the others, still covered in "blood," also spoke to their peers about how they felt and how real it seemed. They felt great satisfaction in having been part of this huge effort to stop drinking and driving in their town.

You can also take part in this effort. This book discusses the problem of drinking and driving. It also describes what others, like the students at Jackson Memorial High, are doing to educate their community about the cost of drinking and driving. Finally, it suggests ways in which you can join others to work together against drinking and driving.

❖ QUESTIONS TO ASK YOURSELF ❖

1) Have you ever been in a car with a drunken driver? 2) Do you think a mock collision like the one Brian's school put on would have an effect on students? 3) How could you help to persuade your friends that drinking and driving can be deadly?

Often people who have lost a loved one in a drunk driving accident speak out in schools to encourage teens not to drink and drive.

chapter

2

THE PROBLEM

"*I was called by the police one night and told that my daughter had been killed in a motorcycle accident,*" *one mother said.* "*But I have three daughters, and they couldn't tell me which one she was. I had to go down to the hospital to identify her. So the ten minutes it took to get there seemed like ten days. When I got there they showed me her jewelry. I saw the ring with the "B" on it, and I knew that it was Becky who had been killed.*"

The pain and the grief of when a young life is taken away is very difficult for parents and family to bear. The rage set in when Becky's parents found out that she had been on a motorcycle with a friend of the family who was drunk when he picked her up. He slammed into a guardrail on the side of the high-way. Becky flew off the bike and landed on her head. The helmet couldn't protect her enough from the impact. She died instantly. The "friend" was only slightly injured.

Becky's parents also found out that he was

driving without a license, it had been revoked. He also had two other drunk-driving convictions in the past few years.

"Our lives were forever crushed when he killed Becky. And that's what he did—he killed her," Becky's mom said. "Now I speak at school programs about not going anywhere with a drunk driver. If Becky hadn't gotten on that bike . . . If he hadn't been drunk . . . All the 'ifs' don't change what happened. I want kids to know that they don't have to do what Becky did."

The facts about drinking and driving show that Becky is not an exception. Many people are hurt or killed by incidents involving drunk drivers.

- Alcohol was involved in 17,461 (44 percent) of 40,115 traffic fatalities (deaths) in 1993.
- 289,000 more people were reported by police to have been hurt in alcohol-related crashes.
- A total of 400,000 alcohol-related crashes were reported by police in 1993.
- Alcohol-related crashes, injuries, and deaths cost the United States at least $46 billion in lost workers, medical costs, damages to property, and other direct costs. Over $5 billion of this goes toward medical care.

- Alcohol-related deaths in 1993 alone resulted in more than 600,000 years of potential life lost.

More than 1.5 million drivers are arrested for driving under the influence (DUI) each year. This is an arrest rate of one driver out of every ninety to ninety-five licensed drivers in the United States. About two in every five Americans will be in an alcohol-related crash at some time in their lives. In fact, alcohol-related highway death is the number one killer of teens and young adults in the United States today.

A lot of people out there are drinking and driving, and many of them are teens. Alcohol is the major cause of all fatal and nonfatal crashes involving teenage driving. The number of deaths from such accidents is frightening. One young driver dies every three hours in this kind of crash.

❖ DRIVING UNDER THE INFLUENCE ❖

Carlos had already had one drunk-driving accident and figured that he had used up his share of bad luck. He had recovered from minor injuries from the accident. No one else was in the car with him, so he felt that the driver re-training program that he was required to attend didn't really apply to him.

"I didn't think it would happen to me again,"

Alcohol affects people differently. If you are a female of light weight drinking on an empty stomach, the alcohol will affect you very quickly.

Carlos said. "I usually drove pretty good even after a six-pack. I wasn't far from home either."

Carlos is now in a wheelchair because of one too many beers, and thinking he could drive "pretty good" when he had been drinking. He is permanently paralyzed from the chest down and only has very little use of his arms and hands.

"I'll never drive again. I can't move out of my parents' house. I'll never be on my own, traveling across the country like I wanted. My life has been completely changed. I didn't learn my lesson the first time."

Carlos also appears at high school programs telling teens about what happened to him. He figures if he stops even one life from being ruined like his was, it will be worth it.

"It's scary, you know? Because I see in their eyes what was in my own even after the first accident. Not me. Maybe someone else, but not me. I'll never end up like this. I used to think that too."

About one-third of high school seniors binge-drink (drink to get drunk) at least once every two weeks, and four percent of those drink daily. Many teens drive drunk. Some may believe that one or a few drinks will not affect their ability to drive, but they are wrong. Alcohol does affect a drinker's body, and impairs his or her judgment.

Each person responds to alcohol differently. Many things affect how your body absorbs alcohol. How much you weigh, whether you are male or female, how much food you've eaten, and how long you have been drinking determine how your body handles the liquor you drink. If you do not weigh a lot, if you are female, or if you are drinking on an empty stomach, you will be affected by alcohol more quickly.

You are considered to be "driving under the influence" of alcohol when your blood alcohol content (BAC) reaches .10 percent. This means that there is roughly one drop of alcohol in your bloodstream to every 1,000 drops of blood.

Most people's blood alcohol content reaches .10 percent after drinking three drinks in an hour. A typical drink is a can of beer, a glass of wine, or a shot of liquor in a drink (this usually equals over one half ounce of hard liquor). However, many drinks contain more than one shot. Wine coolers can equal about one and a half typical drinks.

However, your driving skills are impaired even when you have less alcohol in your body.

Reaction time. To drive well, you need to be able to have a quick reaction time to avoid accidents. Your reaction time starts to slow down when you have a blood alcohol content of .04 percent. If you have to choose from several possible reactions, you start having trouble when your blood alcohol content reaches .03 percent.

Tracking. As you drive, you need to keep your car on your side of the road. This tracking skill is impaired when your blood alcohol content is at .05 percent. If you need to track two or more objects (your car and another's), your ability to track is reduced even further.

Attention. You can focus your attention on a single task when your BAC is as high as .08 percent. But if you need to divide your attention between two or more tasks, such as driving and talking to a friend, you will start to have trouble when your BAC is .05 percent.

Comprehension. Your skill of comprehension, the time it takes for your brain to understand what it sees or hears, is affected at .05 percent BAC. At this level, your vision, control over eye movements, and the ability to merge two images into one suffer. This is when you can start having blurred vision.

Coordination. A blood alcohol content of .05 percent also affects your coordination. In driver performance tests, a blood alcohol content of .08 percent affects the skills needed for steering, speed control, braking, lane tracking, gear changing, and judgment of speed and distance.

As a driver's blood alcohol content increases, so do his or her chances of being in an alcohol-related car crash. By the time the driver's blood alcohol level reaches .06 percent, the likelihood that he or she will be in an accident has doubled. By the time his or her blood alcohol content reaches .10 percent, he or she is twelve times more likely to be in a fatal crash than a nondrinking driver. That is why it is vital that we take steps to reduce the number of people who drink and drive.

In an effort to stop teens from drinking and driving, an amendment to the National Highway Systems Bill was passed. It requires all states to adopt a "zero tolerance" (.00 to .02) blood

If you are arrested and convicted for DUI, you can go to jail, pay a fine, and lose your driver's license.

alcohol content for drivers under the legal drinking age. However, some states have yet to put this amendment into effect. These states often don't prosecute teens who drink and drive as long as their BAC levels don't exceed the states' legal limits. States that don't adopt "zero tolerance" laws for teens under twenty-one will not receive highway funds from the government. Currently, thirty states have such laws.

❖ CONSEQUENCES ❖

People who are arrested and convicted for DUI will face many consequences. They may spend time in jail, face fines of hundreds or thousands of dollars, lose their driver's licenses, and severely increase the cost of their car insurance. They may have caused injury or even death to other people, and they will have to live with that for the rest of their lives. Or they may themselves be killed.

You can make a difference. If you can stop someone who has been drinking from getting behind the wheel of a car, you may save a life. If you stop yourself from driving when you've had alcohol, you may be saving your own life. Knowing the facts and making safe decisions about drinking and driving are powerful forces in working against this problem.

❖ **QUESTIONS TO ASK YOURSELF** ❖
1) How do you suppose Carlos feels, spending his life in a wheelchair? 2) Have you ever done something wrong thinking that you could get away with it, "just this once"? 3) Do you think it would help prevent your classmates from drinking and driving to hear Carlos's story directly from him?

chapter

3

WHAT YOU CAN DO PERSONALLY

*"WE DROVE TO A CONCERT IN THE CITY,
about two hours away," Arturo said. "It was a great
concert, but the evening was almost ruined. My
friend Mo was driving, but he was so drunk that we
almost got in an accident on the way home. I was
really scared. I didn't want to die like that."*

Students Against Driving Drunk (SADD) is an
organization that was founded in 1981. Its goal
is to stop teens from drinking and driving. SADD
and other local and national organizations rec-
ommend making a contract, or pact, with your
parents. It will help you if you find yourself in a
situation like Arturo's. A pact is an agreement by
which you and your parents make a plan and
follow that plan when the need arises.

SADD calls theirs a "Contract for Life." You
can call it anything you want. It is a written
agreement that you and your parents or
guardians sign to make sure you won't have to
ride home with a driver who has been drinking.

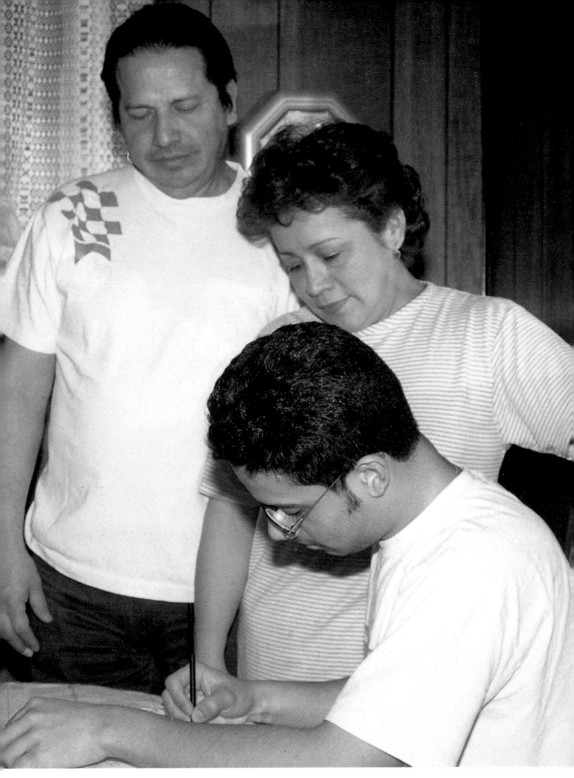

The "Contract for Life" from SADD has saved many lives.

When you have your parents' support, it's easier to make a decision about NOT getting into a car with a drunk driver. When you don't have that support you may feel you have no choice.

Your part of the agreement also concerns situations in which you are the driver who has been drinking and who is responsible for driving others.

In this pact your parents or guardians agree to the same conditions, such as not driving drunk or riding in a car with someone who is drunk.

The agreement may look something like this:

YOUR WRITTEN AGREEMENT

I will call you or _____ (another designated adult, in case a parent is not reachable) no matter what time it is or where I am, if my ride has been drinking, or if I am driving and have been drinking. This does not mean I have permission to drink and call you all the time.

_____
Name

_____
Date

YOUR PARENT'S AGREEMENT

I/We agree to pick you up when you call so that you don't drive after drinking or get in a car with someone who has been drinking. We will

discuss the situation with you the next day. We don't want to punish you, but this doesn't give you permission to drink.

I/We also agree not to drink and drive. One of us will be the designated driver, or if we are with others, we will be sure to arrange safe transportation.

_____
Name(s)

_____
Date

This gives you a way out of a potentially dangerous situation. It gives you and your family a doorway to communicate at a time when a lot of teens or parents close the door. It helps with issues of trust too, giving your parent the opportunity to trust your judgment.

This pact is your agreement to act responsibly. Use it wisely. If you use it as permission to get drunk and then call home for a ride, the pact will become worthless. The more your parents feel they can trust you, the more freedom they will give you.

❖ CHOOSING NOT TO DRINK ❖

Another thing you can do is make a personal decision not to drink. Abstinence from alcohol and drugs is a choice. Some teens don't enjoy drinking, but do it to please their friends.

"Everywhere I go," Sagar said, "there's something to drink or smoke. It's just there, at so many houses, parties, or on kids in school who are dealing drugs. It takes an awful lot to stay away from it."

This is true all over the country. When teens get together, they often feel that they need something to party with. In part, it is because many teens feel awkward; they may believe that alcohol will help them be more relaxed. If you are at a gathering where your peers are drinking, you may be expected to do it too. Saying "no" can bring strong pressure from close friends and popular kids. This is understandable, but there are ways to handle it.

"I made up this story about how drinking inter-feres with my asthma," Angel said. "Then I pop open a can of soda that I brought, and no one seems to bother me too much. There was one time when some-one tried to pour liquor into my soda when I wasn't looking, so now I keep the can in my hand all the time."

If you find yourself in a suddenly uncomfort-able situation, you can always think on your feet. For instance, if you go to a party with some friends and find that almost everyone there is drinking or is high, try to find a person or group of people who is not. You are probably not the

It's important for teens to have friends who don't pressure them to drink.

only person who feels uncomfortable. Try to move around the room until you find a place or group of people where you feel comfortable and are not pressured to drink.

You may be on an athletic team at school or in a dance or sports program outside of school. Some athletes and performers choose not to drink because they don't want alcohol to hurt their performance. You can follow their example. Explain that your seriousness in pursuing a sport or activity makes you choose not to drink. Other teens will usually respect your choice.

"When I arrived at the party, everyone was pretty much plastered," said Anthonio. "I just

*wanted to have a good time and hang out with my
friends, but I did not want to drink, especially during basketball season. I learned my lesson when
I got so drunk at a party once that I couldn't play
in the game the next day. I want to go all the way
with basketball. No way I'm ruining my chances
of being recruited by a university just because
some guys want me to chug a few beers with
them."*

One young woman refused to drink alcohol at
a party because she had promised to baby-sit
her little brother later. When she explained this
and asked for a soda instead, everyone under-
stood, and no one pressured her to drink.

Most importantly, choose friends who support you in your decision not to drink. Plan to
do things that don't involve alcohol. Go to a
movie or go midnight bowling. Rent videos and
watch them at houses where you know alcohol
won't be served. Go out for pizza or spend some
time with your family. You can have a good time
without alcohol.

You always have the choice to stay sober.
However, it's not always easy. If you are someone who has a hard time saying no, especially to
best friends, boyfriends, or girlfriends who want
you to join them, practice a response to get out
of drinking that your friends will accept or
understand.

❖ DESIGNATED DRIVERS ❖

If you and your parents or other adults plan to be in a place where people may be drinking, be smart and plan ahead. At the beginning of the evening, choose a designated driver who will drive everyone home. A designated driver is someone who agrees not to drink so that he or she can drive everyone home safely. That way, someone who has been drinking will not be at the wheel.

❖AVOID BEING AN AT-RISK PASSENGER❖

You also have the right to choose not to ride in a car with someone who has been drinking. This can be hard, because your friend may tell you that he or she didn't have much to drink, or that he or she is not drunk, or may even say, "Don't you trust me?" No one wants to hurt a friend or to have it appear that they don't trust their friend. It may be especially difficult with a boyfriend or girlfriend. But people who have been drinking aren't themselves; alcohol has affected their brains and hurt their ability to drive.

"I got a ride to this party with Greg, this guy from my class" said Rachel. "When we got to the party, Greg headed straight for the alcohol. The party was totally cool, but I was getting worried because Greg kept drinking all night. I knew Greg would be in no condition to drive. I couldn't reach

my parents because they were out, and I didn't want Greg to drive himself home. As we were walking back to the car after the party, I told Greg that my brother, Steve, had the same car as he did, and that I always wanted to drive it. I said, 'Steve was never cool enough to let me drive it, but I know you're way cooler than that.'

"It worked! Greg handed me his keys. He passed out on the ride back to his house. His dad ended up driving me home. He thanked me for not letting Greg get behind the wheel. He said I probably saved Greg from a serious accident. It really made me feel good knowing that I made a difference."

For your friend's sake and your own, do your best to persuade your friend to let you drive. Your friend may be embarrassed by the suggestion, so try to be as casual and supportive as possible. You might say that you want to drive because you just received your driver's license. You can also say you've never driven a car of that make and model and would be grateful if your friend would let you. Or you can say that since your friend never likes the music you choose you will drive while he or she picks the music. But don't get in the car with your friend if he or she insists on driving. If both of you have been drinking, suggest getting a ride with someone else, or getting a cab.

Some teens, trying to prevent friends from

driving drunk have called their friends' parents or even taken away their car keys. These may seem like extreme measures, and these teens may have angered their friends, but they did the right thing. If you are concerned for your friends' lives and that of others, such an action may be sensible. It may save a life.

❖ QUESTIONS TO ASK YOURSELF ❖

1) Does your town have a chapter of SADD? 2) Would you like to sign a "Contract for Life" with your parents? 3) What can you do when there are alcoholic drinks at every party you attend?

Some professional athletes, such as Michael Jordan, volunteer to speak to students about staying straight and sober.

chapter

4

WHAT YOU CAN DO IN YOUR SCHOOL

MANY TEENS ARE DISGUSTED BY THE horrible accidents caused by drinking and driving that claim the lives of their friends and family members. You can work together with others at your school to reduce the incidence of drunk driving.

❖ STUDENTS AGAINST DRIVING ❖ DRUNK (SADD)

You and your friends can start a SADD chapter at your school. Write to the national organization at the following address for information:

Students Against Driving Drunk
P.O. Box 800
Marlboro, MA 01752

SADD will send you starter kits, information, a parent-student "Contract for Life," and other materials to help you organize a chapter in your school.

You can get started by scheduling a meeting at your school with the permission of your school's administration. You'll need an adviser who will be responsible for the group. Ask a teacher or counselor to be your adviser. With your adviser's help, you and your friends can organize the first meeting.

Bring in SADD speakers and members from other chapters to speak. Perhaps a representative from the police department, sheriff's office, or highway patrol will add his or her support against drinking and driving. Invite everyone to this meeting! Ask friends, fellow students, teachers, parents, administrators, community officials, and Board of Education members from your town or city. Local politicians can be invited, too.

Some schools bring in famous athletes who volunteer to talk about staying sober and straight. Students tend to listen to these speakers and take them seriously.

You'll have to devote much of your own time in organizing a chapter. Are you committed? A key group of hard-working people can accomplish a great deal. Try to build a solid, small group. As a group, set your goals. What do you want to accomplish the first month? The first year? Is awareness of the problem of drinking and driving important? Make sure the school administration is involved.

Perhaps the first year you'll concentrate on media campaigns. Local cable and radio stations may be a good way to promote the cause of not drinking and driving. Write articles and letters to the editors of local and regional newspapers to get the word out. Have classmates and parents sign petitions. Send them to your governor, senators, and members of congress to get their commitment for tougher laws. (See chapter 6.)

Get school permission to organize a program in which older students can visit younger students in elementary schools and teach them about the dangers of drinking and driving.

Publicize the goals of your group—get the word out that there's a SADD group that cares about saving lives.

❖ PROJECT GRADUATION ❖

This is a national alcohol and safety program to keep teens sober and alive during graduation. This is a time of the year when many students celebrate with alcohol and then get into their cars. You can encourage your school's student government or another school group to work with the community and school to promote this worthwhile project. You can get information on setting up a Project Graduation program by contacting MADD (Mothers Against Drunk Driving).

Safe Rides for Teens is a program that can be set up in your community for teens to call anytime to get a safe ride home. This program ensures that teens do not have to get into a car with someone who has been drinking.

Make announcements and put up signs in your school promoting "Buckle Up Day." Set up a table at lunchtime before graduation and encourage classmates to sign pledges not to drink and drive or get in a car with someone who has been drinking. Get the word out to "Stay alive, don't drink and drive."

This past year a local high school spent their graduation night under the stars on a cruise ship around New York City. It was sponsored by a community alliance that pledged that no '95 graduate would be a victim of alcohol- or drug-related accidents. It was an alcohol- and chemical-free party, with great food and dancing. The graduates cruised on a warm June night. The students came back to their school around 5 A.M. for breakfast and to find out who had won the grand prizes of televisions, calculators, a refrigerator, and a word processor.

❖ SAFE RIDES FOR TEENS ❖

If you find yourself stranded on a Saturday night and the only ride home is with a drinker, what can you do if your parents aren't available? Safe Rides is a system that teens can put into effect to make sure they will have a safe ride home without endangering their lives. A hot line can be set up through your local town government or police. Teens needing a ride home can call, and parent volunteers can be on hand to pick them up.

Holiday times, proms, and graduations are important times to have this project in place. You'll need help from parents and maybe a local service organization like the Elks or Rotary clubs. Guidelines need to be set up beforehand so that everyone is clear about the program. If you want to set up such a program, speak to your local community leaders or members of local organizations such as the Parent Teacher Association.

❖ ORGANIZE A SCHOOLWIDE RALLY ❖

Talk with a teacher or school counselor about

an in-school program. Bring in speakers who have had bad experiences related to alcohol and driving. Families and friends of victims of drunk-driving accidents may wish to participate in an anti-drunk-driving program. Call your local police department to plan a car-crash demonstration like the one described in chapter 1. Try to arrange for local newspaper coverage of the program.

❖ PEER COUNSELING ❖

Many high schools and middle schools have set up peer counseling programs. Teens are usually selected by teachers. They are then trained to be peer counselors. They help other teens deal with problems. They may act as role models and information givers to younger students. Peer counselors can target special problems such as drinking and driving. Peer counseling can be especially effective because teens are often more willing to listen to one another than to adults.

Perhaps in the past you've felt that you were only one person and couldn't do much to change the world. That's not true! Working in your school in a SADD chapter, helping teens get safe rides, and teaching young kids to be sober and stay alive will always make a difference. You don't have to do it alone—there are usually others who will form a core group to help get things done. Many adults are more than willing to be involved. It just takes one special person with an idea to get the ball rolling.

❖ **QUESTIONS TO ASK YOURSELF** ❖

1) Could you start a chapter of SADD at your school? 2) Can you think of safe and sober ways of celebrating graduation day at your school? 3) Would your parents be willing to volunteer in a Safe Rides for Teens program?

5

WHAT YOU CAN DO IN YOUR COMMUNITY

NEW YEAR'S EVE IS A NIGHT WHEN MANY people drink and then drive home. There's been a growing trend in towns and cities to stop focusing on alcohol on New Year's Eve and to provide other forms of community celebration. First Night activities have sprung up all over the country.

"I had heard about First Night plans from my cousin who lives in another state," said sixteen-year-old Latoya. "It sounded like a good idea, so I persuaded the youth group at my church to get things started."

Latoya's friends at church worked with the adults to make their town's first First Night a success. Events were planned all over town at different times in various places to celebrate the coming of the new year. Not one of the activities included drinking or getting high.

The church started off with a B.Y.O.F. (Bring

Events sponsored by your church or other organizations might attract teens who might otherwise drink.

Your Own Food) party. The teens advertised it in advance by handing out pamphlets in school, at local businesses, and throughout the neighborhoods. The church hall was set up with tables and chairs, with room for a D.J. and dance floor for a dance later in the evening. Almost 200 families turned up. Each brought something to eat (such as a casserole or salad) or something non-alcoholic to drink. The teens persuaded local stores to donate paper plates and other supplies.

After dinner, the townspeople headed to the high school gym for a game of basketball between the staff from the local radio station and the teachers. Local "celebrities" such as the mayor and high school

*principal participated, too. The spectators cheered
enthusiastically. They also enjoyed some fancy ball
handling by a former college All-American who lives
in town.*

*Most of the teens returned to the church hall for
the dance. Some of the parents took a Candlelight
Tour of the most festively decorated homes in town.
The final event was a small fireworks display at
midnight beside the lake.*

*"We were glad to have places to go where we were
not pushed to drink," said Latoya's father. "There
was no pressure to finish the champagne bottle at
midnight or make the host happy by polishing off all
the liquor. Even as adults we have to deal with peer
pressure."*

*"I had fun," Latoya said. "Some of the kids in
town didn't want to come, so they stayed home or
went somewhere else and probably drank. At least we
had choices. We could put the pressure on our friends
to join us and not drink on New Year's."*

You and your friends could start a First Night
program in your town. It doesn't have to be a
large-scale production. Start off small so that
you can handle all the details, and plan only a
few activities the first time. You can plan more
activities the next time. Contact community
groups such as Girl Scouts, Boy Scouts, Jaycees,
fire and police departments, school groups,
local businesses, and government officials. Ask

them to help plan and carry out the program.

It would be best to start a few months in advance. Church and synagogue committees of all kinds may be interested in sponsoring one event. A main group will be needed to oversee the entire plan. See that there are activities for all ages and baby-sitting services available at some places. Young parents may want an hour to themselves to take a Candlelight Tour or dance to a few songs, yet may not want to leave their young children or babies for very long. Older couples may want to hear music from another era, such as big band music. Speak with your friends and classmates about the kind of activities that they might like to participate in.

Whether you live in a small town or on a neighborhood city block, First Night can create a nice feeling of community. It may also keep many people safe and sober on New Year's Eve, a night usually associated with drinking and driving.

❖ STRAIGHT AND SOBER WALK ❖

You can work in your community against drinking and driving at other times of the year, too. Organize a Straight and Sober Walk or a rally in town. You can get permission from local authorities to set up a five-mile or ten-mile walk. Urge friends and other people in town to commit to "walking the distance" to raise awareness

One important step in stopping drinking and driving is to raise
awareness around the problem.

against drinking and driving. Make posters or
signs for marchers to carry. The walk can end at
a local field or park where speakers can share
experiences or ideas on keeping your town safe
from drunk drivers.

❖ OTHER IDEAS ❖

Any event you want to plan in your town can
usually be accomplished through the coopera-
tion of local government officials, police person-
nel, adults, and teens. It takes just one person
with an idea to get it off the ground. You can

appear on local cable television or a radio program to publicize it. Flyers can be printed up, possibly at no cost to you, by supportive shop owners in town. Announcements can be made at religious services and meetings of organizations.

Your idea does not have to be big to be successful. Run a poster contest or bumper-sticker design contest at children's recreation programs in the summer. The design should portray your town working against drinking and driving. You can arrange for the winner to have his or her name printed in the newspaper and to be honored at a government meeting. Try to get a store owner in town to display the winning posters or distribute the bumper stickers.

You may want to start a campaign with the local car dealerships in your county or state. With each car purchased, the new owner will receive a flyer or bumper sticker with a slogan expressing a stand against drinking and driving. The design of this flyer or bumper sticker can also be a community contest. Persuade the mayor and town leaders to pose for newspaper photographers and television camera crews as they place their bumper sticker on their own cars. This will make everyone aware that your town won't stand for having people killed or injured by drunk drivers.

There are many people who will join with you to make your city or town a healthier, safer place to live. All people have a vested interest in keeping themselves and members of their families safe from drunk-driving accidents. You can urge your local newspapers to publicize stories of local people who have had their lives changed dramatically by a drunk driver. These victims or survivors may want to tell their stories to educate others. Local television and radio stations are often willing to have teens plan and carry out programs dealing with these issues.

You can accomplish a great deal in your own community. Even if you live in a huge city, one block or one neighborhood can have its own promotion to warn drinking drivers to "stay off our streets."

If you have ideas and want to make a difference, you can work wonders. You can raise local awareness of the issue significantly. More people will think twice about getting behind the wheel after drinking or getting in a car with a driver who has been drinking. The police may step up their efforts as the public demands that more be done to prevent drunk driving. Your town may develop the reputation as a place to avoid driving in if you are not sober.

What you do could save a life, or a whole family. Maybe your family.

❖ **QUESTIONS TO ASK YOURSELF** ❖
1) What is First Night? 2) How might you

establish a First Night program in your community? 3) Do you know some police officers, government officials, or other adults who might help you?

WHAT YOU CAN DO IN YOUR STATE

THE COMBINED EFFORTS OF SADD AND MADD chapters, and many other citizens around this country have resulted in reducing drunk-driving-related deaths. But there are still too many. More action needs to be taken.

To combat drinking and driving, strong laws are needed, and these laws must be enforced. People of all ages also need to be educated about drinking and driving in order to reduce the number of drunk-driving fatalities.

It is important to gather information so that you are educated enough to speak about the problems of drinking and driving. Read books and articles, write to the organizations listed in the back of this book, and watch television programs that provide up-to-date information on this issue.

As a future or present voter, your opinion is important to your local, state, and federal representatives. Start a petition or get a letter-writing

campaign going with your family and friends in
school or in town when important laws about
drunk driving are to be voted upon.

You can find the local address for your representatives in the state legislature in your telephone
book. Tell your representatives that you want
stronger laws passed or that you want them to
vote for or against a certain bill that is coming
up for a vote. (See the sample letter on page 51.)

There is a movement around the country to
lower the BAC level at which one is considered
legally drunk. Some states have already done
this. California has proved that lowering the BAC
from .10 percent to .08 percent reduces the
number of drunk-driving accidents in the state.
Its fatalities have declined since the law was put
into effect in 1990.

The .10 percent level now in effect in most
states is higher than in most other countries.
Many other countries, including Canada and
Great Britain, have BAC limits of .08 percent.
Most of Australia, Finland, and Norway have
limits of .05 percent. Sweden's limit is .02 percent BAC.

You can make a difference by working to get
government officials to pass stricter laws about
driving drunk. Spread the word about efforts to
lower the legal BAC levels and the need for
stricter laws and enforcement methods to fight
the problem of drinking and driving.

Something as simple as writing a letter to your government representative can make a difference in the fight against drinking and driving.

❖ SAMPLE LETTER ❖

Your Name
Your Address (or School and Its Address)
City, State ZIP code

Date
Name of Person (Representative Doe)
Office Address
Street or Box Number
City, State ZIP code

Dear Representative Doe:

I (We) firmly believe that a very important law needs to be made in this state. The legal limit for a person to be considered too drunk to drive should be lowered from a blood alcohol content of .10 percent to .08 percent.

I (We) think this is an important matter. It has already been proved in California that lowering the blood alcohol content reduces the number of drunk-driving accidents and fatalities. I (We) would like to reduce the number of accidents and fatalities in this state as well.

I (We) request that as my (our) representative, you join with me (us) in fighting the problem of drunk drivers.

Sincerely,

Your name (or family or class or group)

You can write letters to the editors of local and state newspapers pushing for more state-wide efforts to stop the deaths and injuries caused by drunk drivers. The organizations listed in the back of this book can work with you. They can also provide you with information and statistics and make suggestions about whom to contact in the government.

You have the right, as a citizen of this country, to feel safe when you are out on the road. You also have a responsibility not to get behind the wheel after drinking so that you do not become part of the problem. You can work with others against drinking and driving.

❖ QUESTIONS TO ASK YOURSELF ❖

1) Do you believe that the laws need to be changed to put an end to drunk driving? 2) Do you think it would help for states to lower the current BAC level? 3) Would you be willing to write a letter to your state or national representative asking for new laws to be passed?

chapter

7

BEGIN WITH THE FIRST STEP

STARTING OUT TO DO SOMETHING YOU HAVE never done before can be scary. You may be wondering if you can really make a difference. You can. Absolutely, you can do it. And you can get involved in many ways.

Start small if you want. Decide that you will not drive if you have been drinking and will not ride in a car with a driver who has been drinking. Sign a "Contract for Life" with your parents. Write a short letter or call your state representative expressing your concern and explaining your view about stopping drunk drivers.

Get a teacher to be an adviser for a new SADD chapter at your school. Be a leader if you feel comfortable with that. Encourage other students to join. Come up with ideas together for activities you can work on. Help organize a First Night for your town or city. Just one step can get the ball rolling.

Learn all you can about how alcohol affects the body and share this information with friends.

Learn all you can about how alcohol affects drivers. You may find yourself joining in a discussion in the cafeteria about how to deal with a friend who wants to drive drunk. It is important not to be judgmental. Just speak clearly about the facts and share your ideas about how to help.

❖ ALTERNATIVES TO DRINKING ❖

If alcohol is a problem in your school, sit down and analyze the situation. When do students usually tend to drink? Do they usually party on Friday nights or during the weekends? Do many drive after drinking? Ask yourself why your classmates drink. Are they bored and have

nothing else to do? Do they just drink as a way
to relax and relieve tension?

After you have answered these questions,
come up with some ideas for programs or events
to replace drinking as the form of entertain-
ment. What does your school or community
offer as an alternative? If teens aren't interested
in the existing alternatives, then you, your
friends, parents and teachers can try to come up
with new ideas. If most of the drinking is done
during Friday nights or during the weekends,
organize a midnight basketball game. Teens can
release their tensions and frustrations through
physical activity instead of depending on alcohol. Or you can organize a non-alcoholic gathering at someone's house. You and your school can
also ask the town's local movie theater to offer a
discount on tickets to students during this time.

You may be very surprised at how many of
your classmates drink because there is nothing
else to do. Some others drink because of peer
pressure. If they're at a party and everyone else
is drinking, then they feel that they have to drink
as well. If there is an event where teens are not
pressured to drink, many teens will not drink.

Along with this, of course, is spreading
awareness about the dangers of drinking and
driving.

All of these steps can lead you on a journey
of helping many others in working together

against drinking and driving. You can help to improve the quality of people's lives by working to keep the roads safe. If you are active in the fight to end drinking and driving, you can make a difference.

❖ **QUESTIONS TO ASK YOURSELF** ❖

1) Will you decide for yourself never to drink and drive and never to get into a car with someone who has been drinking? 2) Do you think one of your teachers might serve as an adviser to a SADD chapter? 3) Do you think you know all you ought to know about the effects of alcohol on your body? How could you find more information about alcohol and its effects on the body?

GLOSSARY

abstinence Choosing not to drink alcoholic beverages.

alliance A group joined together for a cause.

BAC **(blood alcohol content)** Percentage of alcohol in the blood.

contract A written agreement.

conviction Judged guilty or at fault in breaking a law.

CPR **(cardiopulmonary resuscitation)** Procedure to start a heart beating after it has stopped.

designated driver Automobile driver who has agreed not to drink in order to stay sober to drive.

DUI (Driving Under the Influence) Driving with a blood alcohol content higher than .10 percent.

fatal Causing death.

pact Formal agreement.

petition Written request by a group that an action be taken.

revoke To take back, cancel.

trauma Bodily injury caused by a violent happening.

vested Fully guaranteed right, privilege, or benefit.

zero tolerance New law which requires states to adopt a BAC level of .00 to .02 for drivers under twenty-one.

Organizations to Contact

AAA Foundation for Traffic Safety
1440 New York Avenue NW, Suite 201
Washington, DC 20005
(202) 638-5944

American Council for Drug Education
204 Monroe Street
Rockville, MD 20850
(800) 488-3784

**MADD (Mothers Against Drunk Driving)
National Headquarters**
P.O. Box 541688
Dallas, TX 75354-1688
(214) 744-6233

**National Clearinghouse for Alcohol and
Drug Information**
P.O. Box 2345
Rockville, MD 20852
(800) 729-6686
web site: http://www.health.org

National Commission Against Drunk Driving
1900 L Street NW, Suite 705
Washington, DC 20036
(202) 452-6004

National Council on Alcoholism and Drug Dependence, Inc.
12 West 21st Street
New York, NY 10010
(800) 622-2255

National Highway Traffic Safety Administration
400 7th Street
Washington, DC 20590
(202) 366-0123

National Safety Council
1121 Spring Lake Drive
Itasca, IL 60143-3201
(708) 285-1121

SADD (Students Against Driving Drunk)
P.O. Box 800
Marlboro, MA 01752
(508) 481-3568

IN CANADA:

MADD (Mothers Against Drunk Driving) Canada National Office
6507C Mississauga Road
Toronto, ON L5N 1A6
(905) 813-6233

MADD (Mothers Against Drunk Driving) Toronto
557 Dixon Road, Unit 126
Etobicoke, ON M9W 6K1
(416) 244-1340

OSAID (Ontario Students Against Impaired Driving)
101-264 Queens Quay West
Toronto, ON M5J 1B5
(416) 248-5324

FOR FURTHER READING

Grosshandler, Janet. *Coping with Drinking and Driving*. New York: Rosen Publishing Group, 1994.

——. *Drugs and Driving*, rev.ed. New York: Rosen Publishing Group, 1994.

Newman, Susan. *You Can Say No to a Drink or Drug—What Every Kid Should Know*. New York: Putnam Publishing Group, 1986.

"Peer Pressure—The Party's Over But the Painful Memory Lingers," in Motion—The Student Guide to Safe Driving. Northbrook, IL: General Learning Corporation, 1990.

Stearn, Marshall B., Ph.D. *Drinking and Driving, Know Your Limits and Liabilities*. Sausalito, CA: Park West Publishing Co., 1985.

INDEX

**DRINKING
AND DRIVING**

Mothers Against Drunk Driving
(MADD), 35, 48

N
National Highway Systems Bill,
19–20
New Year's Eve, 40–43

P
passenger, at-risk, 29–31
peer counseling, 38–39
peer pressure, 26–28, 42, 55
petition, 35, 48
police, 7–9, 46
    help from, 34, 37, 42–43, 44
problems, dealing with, 38
programs, anti-drunk-driving
    community, 40–46, 53
    in-school, 36–37, 53
        goals, 34
        speakers, 34
Project Graduation, 35–37
Project Prom, 10

prom, 7, 9, 10, 37

R
responsibility, 24, 52

S
Safe Rides, 37
saying "no," 25–28
state representatives, 48, 49, 53
Straight and Sober Walk, 43
Students Against Driving Drunk
    (SADD), 22, 33–35, 48, 53
    adviser, 34, 53
    starting a chapter, 33–35
support, from
    community, 34–35, 37–38
    friends, 28, 30
    parents, 22–25, 37, 53
    school, 34–35

Z
"zero tolerance," 19–20

ABOUT THE AUTHOR

Janet Grosshandler-Smith is a guidance counselor at Jackson Memorial High School, Jackson, New Jersey.

She earned a B.A. at Trenton State College, New Jersey, and followed soon after with an M.Ed. from Trenton while teaching seventh-grade English.

Ms. Grosshandler-Smith is the author of several books, including *Coping with Verbal Abuse, Coping with Drinking and Driving, The Value of Generosity,* and *Coping with the Death of a Parent.*

The author lives in Jackson with her husband, Rudy Smith, and their four sons, Nate, Jeff, Mike, and Rudy. She is also able to squeeze in time for running and reading.

PHOTO CREDITS: Cover photo © Image Bank/Obremski; pp. 2, 36, 54 by Maria Moreno; pp. 6, 23 by Olga M. Palma; p. 10 © Impact Visuals/Ricky Flores; p. 12 © A/P Wide World; p. 16 © Impact Visuals/Stephanie Rausser; p. 20 © International Stock/Earl Kogler; pp. 27, 41 Lauren Piperno; p. 32 © A/P Wide World; p. 44 © A/P Wide World; p. 50 by Katherine Hsu.

PHOTO RESEARCH: Vera Amadzadeh

DESIGN: Kim Sonsky